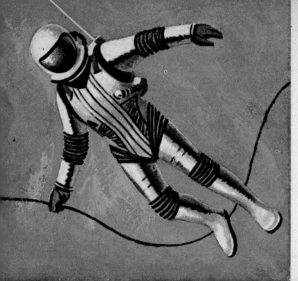

THE HOW AND WHY WONDER BOOK OF
PLANETS AND INTERPLANETARY TRAVEL

Written by
DR. HAROLD J. HIGHLAND
Associate Professor,
Chairman of the Department
of Business Administration,
College of Business Administration,
Long Island University

Illustrated by
DENNY McMAINS

Editorial Production:
DONALD D. WOLF

Edited under the supervision of
Dr. Paul E. Blackwood
Washington, D. C.

Text and illustrations approved by
Oakes A. White
Brooklyn Children's Museum
Brooklyn, New York

WONDER BOOKS · NEW YORK
A Division of GROSSET & DUNLAP, Inc.

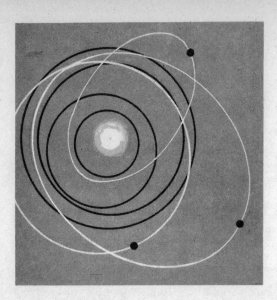

Introduction

Are you on the waiting list for a rocket trip to the moon or one of the planets? You may not have long to wait, for it has already been shown that men can be sent to outer space and returned safely to earth. It is a goal of scientists to extend space explorations with rockets to the moon and beyond, with and without astronauts.

Successes in space exploration are based on the proper application of scientific facts and principles relating to the laws of motion, the mechanics of flight, outer atmosphere, the planets and our solar system, and rocket fuels. *The How and Why Wonder Book of Planets and Interplanetary Travel* deals with many such facts and principles in an easy-to-understand way. Future flights into space will build on this knowledge and thus add new knowledge.

This intriguing book also explores the problems faced by scientists as they try to accomplish man's age-old dream of probing outer space. Can we use nuclear power for rocket fuel? How can we navigate a spaceship? Why are spaceships needed? Can man live on the moon? Answers to these and a multitude of other questions bring the reader up-to-date on space information. At the same time, further questions are propounded — ones for which scientists still seek answers. Thus is curiosity stimulated, and the work of science goes on.

If you are a hopeful candidate for a rocket trip, or merely an armchair observer of such events, you will find *The How and Why Wonder Book of Planets and Interplanetary Travel* a significant reading experience.

Paul E. Blackwood

Dr. Blackwood is a professional employee in the U. S. Office of Education. This book was edited by him in his private capacity and no official support or endorsement by the Office of Education is intended or should be inferred.

Sixteenth Printing

Contents

ANDROMEDA

MILKY WAY

SOLAR SYSTEM

Shaping the Space-Age Dream

Man has always looked for new lands, new mountains, new worlds to conquer. For some, there was a practical reason, such as searching for gold, or for an even more precious commodity — freedom. For

Why should we explore space?

others, there was the adventure and romance of being the first man to fly across the ocean or the first man to explore an unknown cave.

Ever since early history, man has been curious. First, he explored his cave, then the land, next the sea and

SMALL MAGELLANIC CLOUD

NGC 598

LARGE MAGELLANIC CLOUD

The universe in which we live is so vast that we still have not discovered exactly how big it really is. Throughout the universe there are millions of galaxies similar to the one shown here. Our earth and sun — in fact, our entire solar system — is but a minute part of our galaxy. There are more than 100 billion stars in our galaxy and many astronomers believe that there are other planets, in addition to those in our solar system, that are revolving around these distant suns.

PLUTO

SATURN

EARTH MERCURY

JUPITER VENUS ASTEROIDS

MARS

URANUS

NEPTUNE

eventually the air. Today, man stands at a new frontier — space and space travel.

As we go up into the air over the earth, **What is space?** we will not find any road sign along the way saying, "You are now entering space." Actually, once we leave the ground we are in space. The airplanes that fly overhead are in space. But they are only at the very bottom of space. Today, man is interested in *outer space*.

Although scientists have not agreed upon where outer space begins, there are many who feel that once we are about 600 miles above the earth, we are at the bottom fringe of outer space. If this is the bottom, where is the top?

The top or farthest reaches of outer

space is millions and millions of miles away. No matter how far away from the earth we go, we would still be in outer space. In effect, we would be traveling through the universe (U-ni-verse). The universe is the biggest thing we can picture. Everything we know of is in the universe — our earth, the sun, the very distant stars. Therefore, no matter how far out we go from earth, either by exploring with our telescopes or flying in a spaceship, we would always be in the universe and never reach the end of outer space.

The dream of leaving the earth and reaching another world can be traced back in history to the second century

When did man first dream of space travel?

A.D. At that time a Greek, Lucian of Samos, wrote a fantasy about a man who was carried to the moon by a water-spout during a storm. In his second story about space, Lucian's hero flew to the moon with a pair of wings he had made himself.

The moon was the obvious destination for such fantasies because it is so large and has clearly visible markings, which could be thought of as land and sea areas. But for the next 1,400 years, the dream of reaching the moon was abandoned. During this period men believed that the earth was the only world that had ever been created, and that the sun, moon and stars were there to give light and comfort to the earth.

It was not until some 300 years ago, when the famous Italian astronomer Galileo looked through his telescope and told about the other worlds he saw,

that men realized there were other worlds in addition to our earth. Again, they began to dream of reaching these worlds.

In 1634, there appeared a story about a journey to the moon by Johannes Kepler, the German astronomer who discovered how the planets moved about the sun. Although Kepler was a scientist, he transported his hero to the moon by "magic moon people" who could fly through space. Kepler did include a detailed description of the surface of the moon, which he had seen through his telescope.

After Kepler's book, there were many others about space travel and voyages to the moon. They were mostly fantasies, but some contained attempts at scientific reasoning. The first serious discussion of space travel was written in 1640 by Bishop Wilkins of England. It contained a description of physical conditions on the moon and discussed ways in which man could possibly live on the moon. The first man who wrote about a rocket as a spaceship was the noted Frenchman, Cyrano de Bergerac. In his *Voyage to the Moon* and *History of the Republic of the Sun,* he had his space travelers flying to the moon and the sun inside a rocket.

When these books were written about 300 years ago, no one seriously thought that it would be possible to fly through space. It was not until Jules Verne, the French novelist, wrote his story *From the Earth to the Moon* in 1865 that any attempt was made to apply known scientific principles to the space vehicle. By the time that H. G. Wells, the English author, wrote *The First Men on the*

Moon in 1901, man was already at the beginning of a new era in the development of air travel and the conquest of space.

The Earth and Its Atmosphere

What is the atmosphere? The *atmosphere* (AT-mos-phere) is a mixture of gases that surrounds the earth. It is composed of oxygen, nitrogen, carbon dioxide and other gases. Scientists have divided the atmosphere into four layers or levels. Closest to the earth, up to a height of about 10 miles, is the *troposphere* (TROP-o-sphere). This layer contains nine-tenths of all the air surrounding the earth. It is in this layer that our clouds are formed and our weather is made.

The second layer, the *stratosphere* (STRAT-o-sphere), which starts 10 miles up and extends to about 50 miles, contains much less air than the troposphere. Here it is very difficult to breathe, since there is very little oxygen. Above this layer is the ionosphere (i-ON-o-sphere), which extends to 600 miles above the earth. In this layer there is very little air, and it would be impossible to live in the ionosphere for a few minutes without extra oxygen needed for breathing. Furthermore, the sky around you at this level appears black even when the sun is shining.

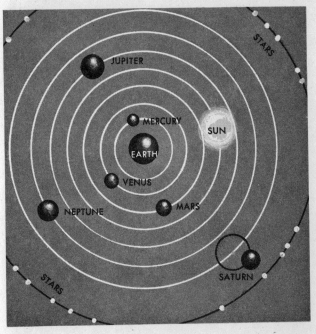

In the second century A.D., the Greek astronomer Ptolemy believed the sun and planets revolved around the earth.

Galileo built his first telescope in Italy in 1610.

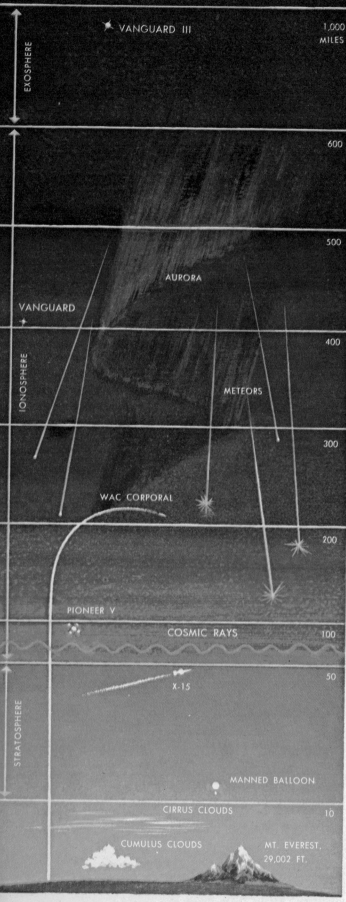

EXOSPHERE	VANGUARD III ★
	1,000 MILES
	600
	AURORA 500
IONOSPHERE	VANGUARD ✦ 400
	METEORS
	300
	WAC CORPORAL
	200
	PIONEER V
	COSMIC RAYS 100
	50
STRATOSPHERE	X-15
	MANNED BALLOON
	CIRRUS CLOUDS 10
	CUMULUS CLOUDS MT. EVEREST, 29,002 FT.

The air between earth and outer space is the atmosphere.

Finally, at 600 miles up and beyond to the far reaches of the universe is the exosphere (EX-o-sphere). This layer contains practically no gases or air and is very, very dark. The exosphere extends out beyond the moon, sun and distant stars.

Man has been probing space ever since

How have we probed the near-reaches of space?

he first turned his eyes skyward to observe the sun, moon and stars. It was not until 1610, however, when Galileo developed his telescope, that man really began to explore beyond the earth. While the telescope provided much information about the heavens, it is only recently that we have obtained detailed information about the space surrounding the earth.

We gathered this information in many ways. First, astronomers used the spectroscope (SPEC-tro-scope) with their telescopes to determine the composition of the stars. The spectroscope is an instrument which uses a prism to separate light rays into their colors. Every element in nature emits a special combination of colors when very hot. The combination for each element is as distinctive as a fingerprint. Each star, like our sun, is very hot and emits rays of light. Therefore, by analyzing these color combinations, it was possible to determine the substances which exist in the stars.

Radio telescopes have provided us with more information than the large 200-inch telescope at Mount Palomar, California. To use a radio telescope, we send radio signals into space, aiming at

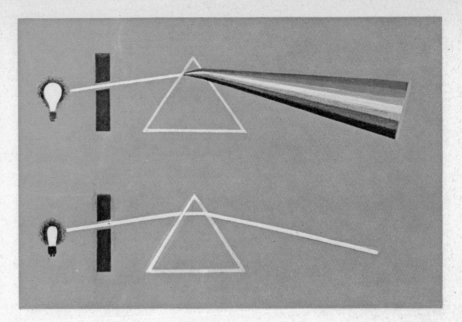

The light from our sun or an ordinary lamp, when it passes through a prism, is refracted (broken up) into an array of colors like a rainbow. But when light from a lamp filled with a single chemical passes through a prism, only the color emitted (given off by the chemical in the bulb) passes through the prism and is not refracted. Astronomers, by studying these light arrays, or spectrums, can determine what chemicals exist in the stars far away from earth.

some part of the sky. These waves bounce back from any object in the sky, such as the moon or a star, in the same way as a ball bounces back to you when you throw it against a wall. The telescope picks up these waves, and scientists, by studying the time it took the waves for their entire trip, can plot surface maps of the heavenly bodies.

To gain even more information about space, men have flown into the stratosphere and into the lower levels of the ionosphere. The American X-15 rocket plane has already been piloted at heights of nearly 70 miles above the earth. More than a score of space flights by American and Soviet astronauts orbiting the earth within the outer limits of the atmosphere have extended our knowledge of space to approximately 1,000 miles from the earth.

Rockets fired into space, as well as artificial satellites carrying a variety of delicate instruments, have probed and sent back to earth a large amount of information on phenomena of the upper atmosphere.

What are cosmic rays? Our sun is a massive, intensely hot body that is composed mainly of two gases — helium and hydrogen. Inside the sun these gases are pressed together under great pressure. The pressure is so great that the atoms, or basic chemical elements in the helium and hydrogen gases, are crushed together.

This crushing together of the atoms results in a tremendous release of energy, which is given off as heat, light and other rays. Cosmic rays are one of these other rays and they travel at a very, very high speed. These rays spread out from the sun in all directions and some reach the earth.

What is the danger of cosmic rays? Exposure to a large amount of cosmic rays would result in severe burns or even death. These rays destroy body tissue and the blood cells in our bodies. Fortunately, only a small portion of these rays reach us here on earth. Many of these rays are trapped thousands of

miles above the earth; a very minute amount come through to us. However, as we go into space we will be exposed to this increased amount of cosmic rays, or cosmic radiation.

What are Van Allen belts? Satellites have sent back information that the earth is surrounded by a huge swarm of high-speed, electrically charged atomic particles, beginning about 2,000 miles from the earth and extending 50,000 miles out into space. These particles form a huge doughnut-shaped belt, with the earth at the center of the "doughnut." This belt, known as the Van Allen radiation belt, was named after its discoverer, Dr. James Van Allen. No one knows where all the thousands of billions of particles come from, but most of them come from the sun. The orbital flights of American and Soviet astronauts have been well below the innermost boundary of the Van Allen belt. However, the radiation will be a danger to humans during the first hours of journeys to the moon and planets. The walls of today's spacecraft give partial protection to astronauts, and scientists are working on ways to eliminate the danger of radiation.

Every so often, giant eruptions, called flares, shoot out from the surface of the sun, flinging vast numbers of atomic particles toward the earth. These storms of particles would endanger the lives of astronauts, should they lack proper protection. Scientists are trying to learn how to predict solar flares so that an astronaut outside of his spacecraft, perhaps exploring the surface of the moon or "walking" in space, may be warned to return to safety.

What is space debris? Traveling at high speed throughout the universe are pieces of metal (mostly iron and nickel) and rock called *meteoroids* (MEE-tee-or-oids) by astronomers. Only about two of every thousand meteoroids are larger than a grain of sand. Most are probably no larger than this letter "o." A very few range from the size of a pebble to the size of a bus. The big meteoroids may weigh more than a hundred tons. (Astronomers also call meteoroids *space debris*.)

About 8 billion meteoroids, traveling at speeds up to 160,000 miles per hour, enter the earth's atmosphere every day. Within it they are called *meteors*. Speeding through our atmosphere, they strike atoms of air and create enough heat to burn up. Rarely, a large meteor may pass through the atmosphere and strike the earth. Those that do are called *meteorites*.

Any meteoroid that strikes a spacecraft is also called a meteorite. A sand-grain-sized meteoroid vaporizes, burning a tiny pit in a spacecraft's outer wall. A pebble-sized meteoroid would punch a hole through a spacecraft, and a large one would entirely demolish the craft.

Nevertheless, scientists feel that a spaceship will not have any difficulty with meteoroids. There is only about one chance in ten thousand that a craft in flight from the earth to the moon would encounter a meteoroid large enough to penetrate an eighth-of-an-inch steel skin of a spaceship. Then, if the ship had several layers of "skin," the chances of any danger from meteorites would be far less.

Casings and fragments of hardware from rockets that have orbited satellites or manned space capsules, as well as satellites that are no longer working, comprise thousands of pieces of space debris now orbiting the earth.

The Worlds Beyond Our World

What is the solar system? The heavenly body with which we are most familiar is the earth. It is one of the nine major planets that revolve about the sun. A *planet* (PLAN-et) is a heavenly body which revolves about a sun. It shines not because of its own light but by the reflection of light from the sun. For example, if you took a lighted electric bulb, it could resemble our sun. Then if you placed a mirror-surfaced ball near it, you would see that the ball was lighted. Actually, the ball is only reflecting the light from the electric bulb.

In addition to the planets there are perhaps 100,000 *planetoids* (PLAN-et-oids), also called *minor planets* or *asteroids* (AS-ter-oids). They differ from the major planets, such as the earth, mainly in size. The largest of these is Ceres, which has a diameter of about 480 miles or about the same size as the state of Texas. Most of the asteroids are small, only about a few miles across, and some are only two feet in diameter.

The next most familiar heavenly body to us is our moon. It is a *satellite* (SAT-el-lite) or a heavenly body that revolves around a larger one in much the same way that the earth is a satellite of the sun. Six of the nine major planets have one or more satellites, or moons, revolving around them. While the earth has only one moon, the planet Jupiter has twelve.

Also traveling around the sun are a number of *comets* (COM-ets). The typical comet has a head and a tail. The head consists of a mixture of gases and small solid particles similar to meteorites. The tail is comprised of many gases. The comet glows as it moves through the heavens.

Many of the comets revolve around the sun in the same manner as the planets, while others come from some distance away in the universe, pass around the sun and then disappear.

Together, the major planets, their satellites, the asteroids, comets, meteorites and our sun form the solar system.

This solar system together with the billions of stars that surround it form our *galaxy* (GAL-ax-y). The galaxy in which we live is called the Milky Way. If we join our galaxy with all the other many billions of galaxies, we then have the universe.

same is true of the sun and earth even though there is no string between them. As the earth and the other planets travel around the sun, they are pulling away from the sun. However, there is another force that is "pulling" on the earth — that is gravity (GRAV-i-ty).

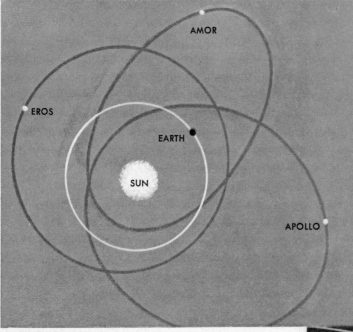

The asteroids that lie between the orbits of Mars and Jupiter revolve about the sun in elliptical orbits just as the planets in our solar system do.

Why do the planets revolve about the sun? If you were able to stand in space millions of miles above the North Pole and observe our solar system, you would find all the planets circling about the sun in a counterclockwise direction, like the hands of a clock running backwards. Why do the planets follow this pattern? If you've ever flown a model airplane in a circle, while holding it with a string, you already know the answer. If you take a model airplane tied to a string, and let it fly in a circle around you, you will find that as long as the airplane travels at the same speed, it stays in the same path and it stays the same distance from you. The

There are nine planets, including the earth, revolving about the sun.

The sun's gravity pulls on the earth and the planets in the same way that the earth's gravity pulls on you. All bodies in the universe have a gravitational attraction on each other.

Gravity is forever exerting its pull. If

How does gravity work?

you throw a ball into the air, it falls to earth because of the pull of gravity. In the seventeenth

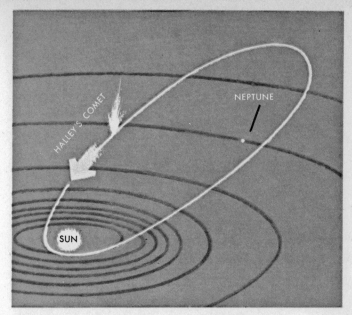

Halley's comet orbits around the sun once in 76 years and it will be visible over the earth in 1986.

century, Sir Isaac Newton of England discovered what we call the "laws" of gravity. He found that all bodies in the universe have an attraction power, and that the power force of gravity depends upon several things. First, the greater the amount of matter or weight of a body, the greater is its gravity pull. For example, the earth has a greater gravitational pull than the moon, just as the sun has a greater gravitational pull than the earth. Second, Newton found that the distance between the bodies affects the strength of this force. Thus, gravity has a stronger pull when the two bodies are closer together than when they are farther apart.

Did you ever spin a top or a gyroscope?

How does _rotation_ differ from revolution?

As the top or gyroscope turns round and round rapidly, it is rotating (ro-TA-ting). Astronomers know that all the planets, including the earth, rotate around their own axis, or an imaginary line drawn through the center of the

13

earth from the North Pole to the South Pole. It is this rotating motion that causes night and day. As the earth spins on its axis, part of it faces the sun and the other part faces away from the sun. One complete rotation takes twenty-four hours or a day. At times, we refer to half a rotation as daytime and the other half as nighttime.

This rotating motion is called *sidereal* (si-DE-re-al) motion by astronomers. Hold a ball in your hand between the thumb and index finger. At the point where the thumb touches the ball, picture the South Pole, and where the index finger touches the ball, the North Pole. Put a chalk mark halfway between the poles. This will be the equator or middle of the earth. Now place another chalk mark near the North Pole. As you rotate the ball and make one complete turn, you will see that the mark at the equator has to travel a bigger distance than the mark near the pole. In other words, the mark at the equator has to travel faster than the mark near the pole since it covers a longer distance.

This is also true on earth. In New York and Chicago, for example, the earth's sidereal motion or speed amounts to 700 miles an hour or 12 miles a minute. At the same time that the earth is rotating, it is also moving around the sun. This movement is called *revolution* (rev-o-LU-tion). One complete trip around the sun is one revolution, or, as we know it, one year. To make this trip the earth travels at a speed of 18½ miles per second. In one hour it covers more than 66,600 miles in space on its orbital trip around the sun.

The planets revolve about the sun in a planetary orbit; that is, they move in an ellipse (el-LIPSE) or elongated circle. To draw an ellipse, stick two thumbtacks into a piece of cardboard about four inches apart. Make a loop of string about four inches long and slip it over the tacks. The loop should not be too taut. Stick a pencil point through the loop and stretch the loop out. Then, holding the

What is a planetary orbit?

The earth's rotation results in day and night as parts of the earth face toward or away from the sun. The earth's revolving in an elliptical orbit about the sun results in the four seasons of the year.

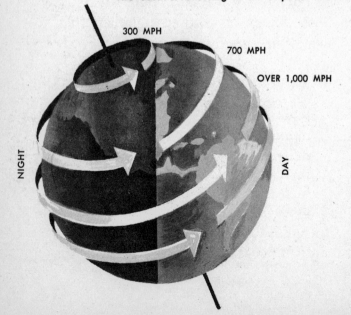

300 MPH

700 MPH

OVER 1,000 MPH

NIGHT

DAY

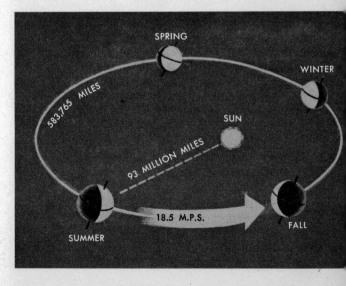

SPRING

WINTER

583,765 MILES

SUN

93 MILLION MILES

18.5 M.P.S.

SUMMER

FALL

pencil in this fashion, move it along the string and draw on the cardboard. You have now drawn an ellipse.

The points where the thumbtacks are placed are called the focal points of the ellipse. It was the German astronomer Kepler who proved that the planets revolve about the sun in an elliptical or planetary orbit and that the sun is located at one of the focal points.

The earth, like the other planets, travels about the sun in an elliptical orbit. At its nearest point, or *perihelion* (per-i-HE-li-on), the earth is 91.4 million miles away from the sun. At its farthest point, or *aphelion* (a-PHE-li-on), the earth is 94.6 million miles from the sun. The average distance between the earth and sun, according to astronomers, is 93 million miles.

Between the orbits of the planet Mars

What is the asteroid belt?

and Jupiter is a space some 350 million miles wide. For many years, astronomers thought that there should be a planet in this space because

it was so large and it left a gap in what they considered the normal spacing between planets. In 1801, astronomers found a heavenly body only about 480 miles wide. They watched it through their telescopes and found that it revolved around the sun like a planet. Several years later they discovered many more "small planets" in this portion of the sky.

Today, we know this region as the asteroid belt. It is believed to include more than 100,000 planetoids or asteroids. Some are ball-shaped, like the earth, while others are like irregular chunks of rock. The largest of the asteroids is Ceres, 480 miles in diameter. Other known asteroids are much smaller. Adonis, Apollo and Hermes are only about a mile or less in diameter.

Between these asteroids and the sun are the *inner planets* — Mercury, Venus, Earth and Mars. The planets beyond the asteroids — Jupiter, Saturn, Uranus, Neptune and Pluto — are known as the *outer planets*. (See illustration, pages 12-13.)

The earth, like the other planets and asteroids, revolves about the sun in an elliptical orbit. You can draw these orbits of our solar system, using a pencil, two thumbtacks and a piece of string.

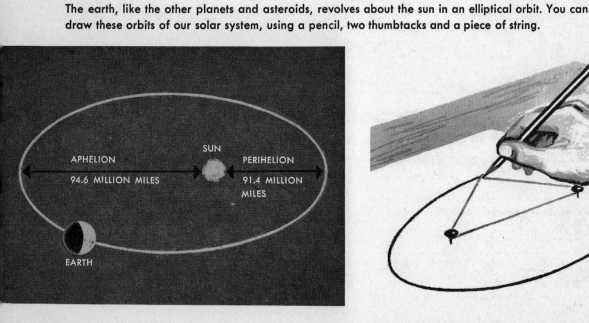

SUN

APHELION
94.6 MILLION MILES

PERIHELION
91.4 MILLION MILES

EARTH

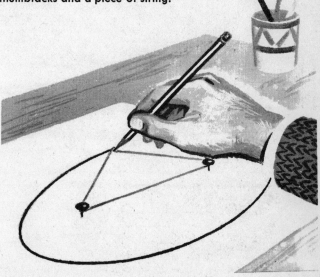

Mercury, the nearest planet to the sun, is also the smallest. It is only slightly larger than our moon — 3,100 miles in diameter as compared with our moon's 2,160 miles. Because of its small size, there is very little gravity as compared with earth. For example, if you weigh 100 pounds on earth, you would weigh only 35 pounds on Mercury.

Why will it be difficult to explore Mercury?

The pull of gravity is what holds the clouds and air around the earth. On Mercury, however, there is no atmosphere because the gravity is so low. Thus, there are no clouds, no rain, no water on that planet.

Mercury completes its orbit around the sun, or makes one full trip in its ellipse, in only 88 earth days. As it takes the planet exactly the same length of time to rotate upon its axis, Mercury always keeps one side facing the sun. Here the temperature reaches almost 800° F., which is hot enough to make lead melt and boil. On Mercury's other side, where the sun never shines, the temperature drops to —460° F. At this very low temperature, it is so cold that oxygen (which we need for breathing) and nitrogen (which we have in our air) would be frozen solid.

The intense heat and extreme cold, the dangerous glare from the burning sun, the lack of water and the low gravity would make it most difficult to explore the surface of Mercury.

The hot sun shines down continually on one side of Mercury; here the heat is so intense that lead would boil.

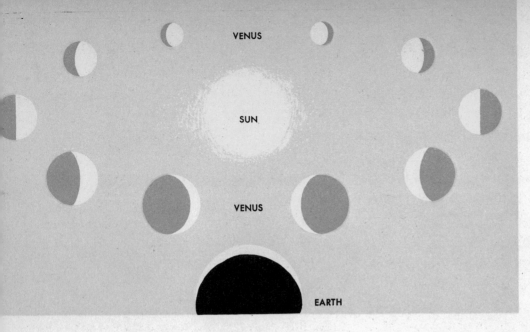

SUN

VENUS

VENUS

EARTH

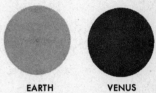

EARTH   VENUS

Like our moon, the planet Venus has phases. It appears as a thin crescent when nearest the earth.

Venus, about the same size as the earth,

What will we find on the planet Venus?

and often called "our sister planet," is also our nearest neighbor in space. At its nearest point, Venus is 26 million miles from earth. It is the brightest of all planets because of the reflection of the sun from its massive clouds. No one has ever seen the surface of Venus — even with the most powerful telescope — since the planet is always completely covered with thick white layers of clouds.

These clouds are not like those we have on earth, which are composed of water vapor, ice crystals and some dust. The clouds of Venus, according to astronomers, consist of large amounts of dust and crystals of frozen carbon dioxide.

The Venus clouds do not change their shape, and this has led scientists to conclude that there are no great oceans and land masses or continents on Venus, as there are on earth. If there were large oceans and land areas, vertical air currents would be formed similar to those on earth; and if these air currents were

present, they would penetrate the cloud cover and cause the clouds to move.

In 1962, the United States space probe, *Mariner II,* passed within 22,000 miles of Venus. Information radioed back to earth indicated that the surface temperature there was as high as 800° Fahrenheit. Russia's *Venus 4* space probe, in 1967, entered the atmosphere of Venus and parachuted instruments to the planet's surface. These measured the temperature of the atmosphere, finding it to range from 104° to 536° F. *Venus 4* also found that the Venusian atmosphere is almost pure carbon dioxide, a fact confirmed by the United States *Mariner V* which swooped to 2,480 miles of the surface of Venus the day after *Venus 4* arrived.

Obviously, the surface of Venus is too hot to support life as we know it. *Mariner II* had found that Venus rotates on its axis in the direction opposite that of the earth's rotation, the Venusian day being as long as 225 earth days. This probably results in winds that blow vast dust storms over Venus's hot, waterless surface. It will be a long time before men find a way to explore Venus.

17

Is Mars another earth? Many space stories have been written about the red planet Mars, because that planet is more nearly like earth than any other planet. Mars is about half the size of earth and is half again as far from the sun than the earth is. Mars rotates at about the same speed as the earth. Its day is 24 hours and 37.4 minutes of earth time. Its year, however, is about twice as long as ours, or 686.7 earth days.

Because it is some 50 million miles farther from the sun than the earth, Mars receives less than half the light and heat from the sun than we do. Its temperature could be tolerated by a spaceman, since it is not too different from that on earth. Around the center of Mars, similar to the equator of earth, the daytime temperature rises to about 85° F., and at night, it drops to somewhat below freezing. At its polar regions, the temperature of Mars is slightly above freezing in the daytime, but it goes as low as −130° F. at night.

Because it is smaller than earth, its gravity is lower. In fact, the gravity pull on Mars is only slightly greater than that on Mercury. Another difference is its atmosphere. While it contains water vapor and carbon dioxide, there is no trace of pure oxygen gas as there is in the earth's atmosphere.

The Martian landscape has fascinated men for centuries. Polar ice caps are visible during the winter season on Mars. During the summer, the ice caps appear to melt and the white surface of the ice disappears. In place of it we find a large green-looking area. Recent explorations of Mars with radio telescopes indicate that these polar caps are not like those on earth. Whereas the earth's polar caps are hundreds of feet thick, the Martian ice caps are about one-twenty-fifth of an inch thick.

The question of why the surface appears green has long puzzled scientists. How could life exist without oxygen in the air to breathe? This has been answered partially by plants we have on earth, lichens. These small plants produce their own oxygen in the daylight and use it at night instead of drawing it from the atmosphere. We do not know if these are the Martian plants or not, but it is believed they might be.

In addition to the polar caps, astronomers have observed large bright areas, reddish in color, which they thought to be deserts, and large dark areas, which they believed to be oceans Today, scientists think that the dark areas are a form of plant life similar to

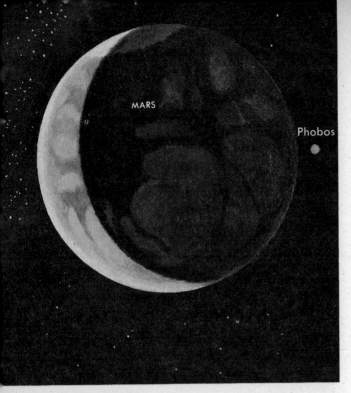

we have no proof that intelligent life, such as man, also exists there. Mars would not be too unfriendly to the spaceman. It is far more inviting than the moon, for there are some indications that Mars is a living world rather than a dead one.

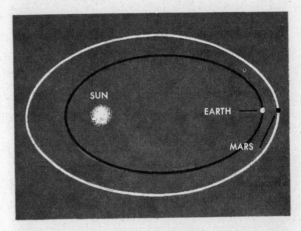

There are advantages in sending a rocket or space-ship to Venus before sending one to Mars. First, Venus is closer to the earth — some 26 million miles as compared with 35 million miles, which is the near-est Mars comes to earth. Second, the earth and Venus are in this close position every 19 months, whereas the earth and Mars are closest only once in 25 months. On the other hand, a space vehicle has to gain speed as it travels from earth to Venus. The earth's speed in orbit (sidereal rate) is 66,000 miles an hour as compared with 78,000 miles an hour for Venus. In a shot at Mars, the space vehicle has to reduce its speed, since Mars' orbital speed is only 54,000 miles an hour, or 12,000 miles slower than earth's orbital speed.

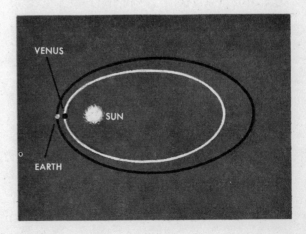

that which is visible at the polar regions during the summer. Scientists also believe that the bright areas are mineral or rock surfaces.

One of the most important reasons why many people believed that intelligent life existed on Mars is the presence of what seemed to be *canals*. Many people believed that some reasoning being, like man, lived on Mars and built the canals in order to irrigate the lands. The canals are the same color as the areas thought to be oceans. Now, with the use of high-powered telescopes, astronomers find that the canals are not so narrow or so straight as was believed. In July, 1965, the United States space probe *Mariner IV* sped past Mars, only 7,400 miles from the planet's surface. Pictures transmitted to earth by *Mariner IV* show that Mars has no surface water and reveal no straight lines that could be artificial canals.

While we accept the possibility that elementary plant life exists on Mars,

Jupiter, the largest of all the planets,

What is the inner core of Jupiter like?

has the shortest "day" as measured by earth time — 9 hours and 55 minutes. It shines brightly in the sky because it is so large, and it is about eleven times greater in size than the earth. There are twelve moons that orbit around Jupiter in an elliptical pattern, just as the planets do around the sun. Four of the moons are as large as, or larger than, our own moon, which is 2,160 miles in diameter. The other eight moons of Jupiter vary in size from about 15 to 100 miles in diameter.

Several large gaseous layers of clouds surround the surface of Jupiter. Some are composed of poisonous ammonia and methane gases, and others consist of hydrogen and helium gases, like those of the sun. Within one of these large cloud layers is a giant red area — "the red spot of Jupiter," as astronomers call it. This red spot is somewhat larger than the earth and it was first seen in 1875. We do not know what makes it red, but we have noticed that it has become fainter and fainter every year. Some day it may disappear entirely, or maybe a spaceship will reach it to discover why it is red.

Circling the sun at a distance more than five times the distance from the sun to the earth, Jupiter receives very little light or heat from the sun. Its surface is believed to be a thick mass of ice that never melts. The surface temperature is about —215° F., and it never rises much above that extremely cold level.

For many years, Jupiter has been called a "gas giant," for it was impossible to determine whether or not it was really solid below the ice. In recent years, using radio telescopes, astronomers have found that the inner core of Jupiter is composed of hot molten material. How can the outside covering be solid ice when the inside is very hot? Wouldn't the heat melt the ice? But astronomers are sure of the ice covering and the hot molten material inside. What they do not know is what is in between. Some believe that there is an insulating material separating the hot material inside from the ice outside.

Jupiter, the largest and the fastest-rotating planet, completes one rotation in less than 10 earth hours.

JUPITER

· EARTH

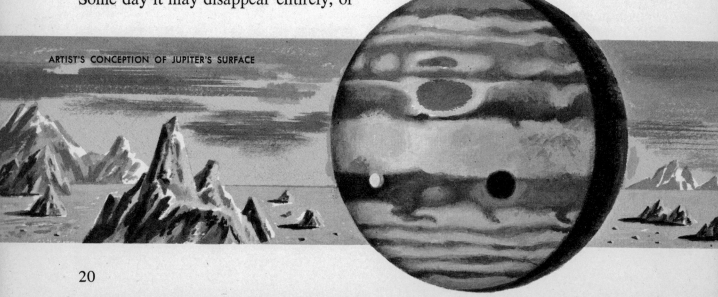

ARTIST'S CONCEPTION OF JUPITER'S SURFACE

Others believe that there is a layer of water between the two. Perhaps in the future you may learn the answer after a spaceman has explored Jupiter.

Because of its tremendous size, the gravity pull of the planet Jupiter is 2.64 times greater than that on earth. This means that a spaceman who weighed 200 pounds on earth would weigh 528 pounds on Jupiter. It also means that it would require much more power to blast off in a spaceship from Jupiter than it does from earth.

Saturn is similar to Jupiter in many ways. It, too, con-

What lies beyond Saturn's rings?

sists of a molten core that is surrounded by an ice cover thousands of miles thick. It also has an atmosphere filled with deadly methane and ammonia gases. However, this atmosphere

The rings of Saturn, visible only through a telescope, appear at different angles each year. When they are tilted toward earth, Saturn's brightness increases.

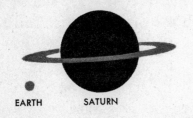

EARTH   SATURN

is much more stable than Jupiter's; that is, it is more like our own sky on a calm, clear day as compared with our sky during a violent, windy thunderstorm.

Only slightly smaller than its sister "gas giant," Saturn is almost twice as far as Jupiter is from the sun. Little of the sun's heat or light reaches the surface of Saturn. The surface temperature of the planet is believed to be about −240° F.

Like Jupiter, Saturn rotates quickly. Its day is equal to 10 hours and 12 min-

utes of earth time. Its year, or the length of one complete revolution around the sun, is about 29½ earth years.

There are two strange features about this planet. First, it has nine moons, the largest of which, Titan, is about the size of Mercury. But unlike the planet Mercury, Titan has a very small atmosphere. Furthermore, one of the moons of Saturn revolves from east to west, or clockwise, around the planet, while the other eight moons revolve in the normal solar system direction, counterclock-

Comparison in size of Saturn's moons with our moon.

TITAN

EARTH'S MOON

IAPETUS

RHEA

DIONE

TETHIS

PHOEBE   HYPERION   MIMAS   ENGELADUS

wise. Why this moon behaves in this manner, no one knows. It is one of the mysteries of astronomy and space.

The second strange feature about this planet is its rings. Imagine a grapefruit cut in half; one part is placed cutside down on a very large plate and the other side is set against the bottom of the plate directly below the top half. This is the way the rings appear around Saturn.

Saturn's rings, which are much brighter than the planet itself, are composed of millions of small solid particles and ice crystals. The rings around the center of Saturn start at about 7,000 miles from the surface. There are several distinct rings and the farthest one away from the planet measures about 10 thousand miles in diameter. The whole ring system measures 170 thousand miles in diameter. Astronomers had believed that these rings were about 50 miles thick, but recent studies have put the thickness at only 10 miles.

The uncertainties about the planet and its great distance from the earth mean that no spaceship will reach Saturn until we have progressed far beyond our current technological levels in space travel.

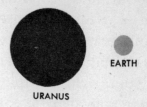

URANUS   EARTH

When first seen by astronomers in 1690,

Where is our sun only a brilliant star?

Uranus was thought to be a star. It was not until 1781 that Sir William Herschel of England discovered that Uranus was a planet that revolved about our sun just as the earth does. Uranus is twice as far as Saturn is from the sun or twenty times that of the earth from the sun. From that faraway distance, we believe that our sun looks like a bright star in the sky.

Unlike all the other planets, Uranus rotates on an imaginary axis that almost points directly at the sun. It would be much the same as if our earth were turned so that the North Pole would be almost pointing at the sun. In rotating on this axis, the north pole of Uranus faces the sun for almost twenty years. Then as the planet shifts, the rays of the sun move over the equator and shine over the south pole of Uranus for about

Uranus rotates strangely on its axis with the sun shining on the planet's north pole for 20 years. The planet then turns and its south pole faces the sun for 20 years.

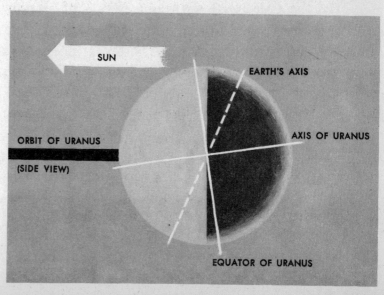

SUN

ORBIT OF URANUS

(SIDE VIEW)

EARTH'S AXIS

AXIS OF URANUS

EQUATOR OF URANUS

twenty years. Because of its great distance from the sun, little heat reaches that planet. The surface temperature is believed to be about −300° F.

Although Uranus is four times larger than the earth, it is not as dense or as heavy as the earth. Its surface gravity is slightly less than the gravity on earth. In addition, its atmosphere, or the gases surrounding the planet, are poisonous ammonia and methane.

Neptune, as it would be seen from one of its moons.

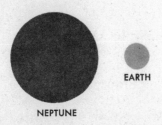
NEPTUNE   EARTH

After Uranus was discovered, astronomers were puzzled by its orbit around the sun. They knew that all heavenly bodies have a gravitational attraction or pull. Both the French astronomer Urbain Leverrier and the Englishman John C. Adams decided that there must be another planet beyond Uranus that was attracting it with its gravitational pull. Only in that way could the orbit of Uranus be explained. In 1848, the German astronomer Johann Galle located the new planet, Neptune, with his telescope exactly where Urbain Leverrier had predicted it would be.

How did gravity help astronomers discover Neptune?

Neptune is the outermost of the four "gas giants" and is more than three times larger than the earth. Its surface gravity is almost one-and-a-half times greater than on earth — and is greater than any planet's surface gravity except

Jupiter's. Like its sister "gas giants," it is covered with ammonia and methane gas clouds over an icy surface. Astronomers believe that the temperature on Neptune's surface is about −330° F.

In some ways, Neptune and Uranus are more similar than the earth and Venus. The main difference between these two planets is that Neptune is somewhat colder and slightly smaller. It also appears bluish, while Uranus has a greenish hue when observed with a telescope. Little is known about the surface of either of these two distant planets, and we can only guess that the surface would be somewhat the same as that on Jupiter or Saturn.

After Neptune was discovered, astronomers found that they still could not fully explain the orbit of Uranus. There had to be another heavenly body which was exerting a gravitational pull on Uranus so that it followed its strange orbit around the sun. A search was begun to find the missing planet. The letter X, used by mathematicians to signify an unknown quantity, was used as the name of the missing planet during the search.

Why is Pluto called Planet X?

PLUTO

EARTH

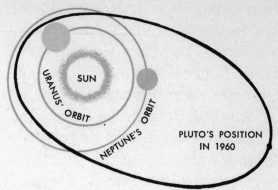

Both Pluto and Neptune revolve about the sun, but their orbits overlap and the planets cross each other twice in one complete revolution. A collision is possible, but it is thought unlikely since the nearest the two planets get to each other is 24 million miles.

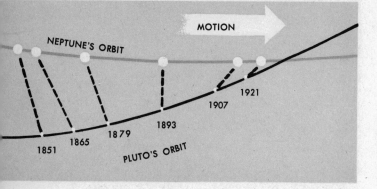

NEPTUNE'S ORBIT

MOTION

1851 1865 1879 1893 1907 1921

PLUTO'S ORBIT

In 1900, the American astronomer Percival Lowell started on his long search for Planet X. He directed much of the search and, finally, in 1930, the missing planet was found by Clyde Tombaugh. This planet was labeled "PL" for Percival Lowell and was called Pluto.

Pluto is amazing in many ways. It is more than 3½ billion miles from our sun. Its year, or one revolution around the sun, takes more than 248 earth years. The planet is somewhat larger than Mercury, and its interior is more like the earth's than its neighboring "gas giants."

In studying Pluto, astronomers found that its orbit cut across Neptune's. Will they ever collide? Many years were spent to answer this question. It was found that the difference in speed at which these two planets revolve about the sun has prevented them from colliding thus far. It takes a considerable amount of mathematics to make these calculations. Maybe some day, millions of years from now, the two planets will collide. It can be computed mathematically if you have the years to work on the problem.

How do astronomers measure distance? Because of the very large distances they must measure in space, astronomers have developed special units of measure. In this way they can avoid using all those zeros, such as we encounter in measuring the distance of Pluto to the sun — 3,500,000,000 miles. One of the basic astronomical units is a *light year*.

Light travels at the speed of 186,000 miles per second. In one day a ray of light travels over 16,000,000,000 miles. In one year it travels 5,880,000,000,000 miles. To the astronomer, this is one light year.

So instead of writing this number with all the zeros, the astronomer merely writes "one light year."

How far away are the stars? The convenience of the light year unit of measure is readily seen when we start talking about distances to the stars. You have looked up into the sky at night and seen the stars. But what is a star? A star is a heavenly body that shines by its own light. That means it must be very hot to give off heat and light, just like our sun. Actually, our sun is a star; it is the nearest star to us — 93 million miles away.

Aside from our sun, how far is the nearest star? That star, called Proxima Centauri, is almost 25 trillion miles away. To the astronomer this is 4¼ light years.

The next nearest star is Alpha Centauri, and it is 500 billion miles farther away than Proxima Centauri. Alpha Centauri is in the constellation, or star group, known as *Centaurus,* and it has the same brightness as our sun. However, it is so far away that it appears as a mere dot in our sky.

A *galaxy* is a cluster, or group, of stars.

What is a galaxy? Our solar system is part of such a group, or galaxy, in which there are more than 100 billion stars like our sun. The diameter of our galaxy is estimated to be 10 million light years, and remember that each light year is almost 6 million million miles.

More than a century ago, Joseph von

Is there life on the other planets? Littrow, an astronomer in Vienna, suggested that we build many tremendous bon-

Our galaxy (our solar system and billions of stars) is a huge flat spiral about 475 million billion miles long. Below, a side view, and at the right, a top view. The cross indicates the position of our solar system.

fires in the Sahara Desert in Africa. These fires would be a signal to any beings living on Mars. While the fires were never built, the speculation about life on Mars, on Venus and on the other planets has continued.

There are many people who believe that no intelligent, reasoning forms of life can exist in the choking atmosphere of Venus, or on the arid surfaces of Mars or, in fact, anywhere else in our solar system. Others, however, feel that life in some form may exist, but it would certainly be different from the life forms we know on earth. Thus far, there has been no definite proof to support the views of either side.

Early in 1961, scientists at the National Institute of Health in Washington, D. C. announced that they had started to grow "life" that they believed came from another world. These "bugs," as they called them, were little twisted rods about eight- to sixteen-millionths of an inch long. They found this "life" inside a meteorite that fell at Murray, Kentucky in 1950. This "life," according to the scientists, was unlike anything we have ever found on earth.

Another group of scientists from Fordham University and Esso Research and Engineering Company in New York City announced at the same time that they, too, found "other-world life." They discovered waxy compounds inside a fragment of a meteorite that fell near Orgueil, France in 1864.

Although there are some scientists who feel that these two findings are now definite proof that life does exist elsewhere in the solar system, there are many others who do not accept these "proofs" of life. They feel that the waxy compounds are too similar to those we have on earth and that the meteorite became contaminated over the years, thus producing this strange substance. They also feel that the little twisted rods of life, which the Washington scientists presented, come from high up in our own atmosphere. Not until man is able to explore space more thoroughly and travel through it in his own spaceship, will he be able to obtain a definite answer about life on other planets.

Key to Planetary Exploration—
the Spaceship

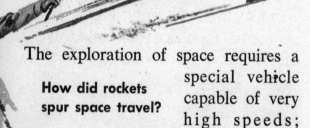

The Chinese used "war" rockets in A.D. 1232.

The exploration of space requires a special vehicle capable of very high speeds;

How did rockets spur space travel?

that is, thousands of miles per hour. This space-exploring vehicle, or spaceship as we call it, is merely the next step after the giant rocket. Rockets have a long history of use for entertainment and war. Their greatest development came, however, when scientists realized that rocket power was needed to explore space and to enable spaceships to reach the moon and eventually the planets.

The earliest attempt to use rocket power to fly is supposed to have taken place more than 1,000 years ago in China. This early "spaceship" was a bamboo chair to which forty-seven rockets, or large firecrackers, similar to those shot into the air on the Fourth of July, were attached. The pilot of this early spaceship was a Chinese mandarin named Wanhu. When the firecrackers were ignited, the chair was supposed to shoot up into the air. Unfortunately, when they were ignited, Wanhu and his "ship" disappeared in a cloud of smoke and flame.

In their attack on Washington, D. C. in 1814, the English used a war rocket, which was invented by Sir William Congreve. The American Army was routed

"And the rockets' red glare, the bombs bursting in air . . ." was inspired by the British rocket bombardment of Fort McHenry in 1812.

Dr. Robert H. Goddard, father of American rocketry, built and fired rockets more than forty years ago.

and the British captured the capital. Several weeks later, these rockets were used during the British bombardment of Fort McHenry, near the city of Baltimore, Maryland. This famous event is referred to in the United States National Anthem, *The Star-Spangled Banner* — "And the rockets' red glare, the bombs bursting in air . . ." The rockets failed this time and Fort McHenry did not surrender.

It was not until early in the twentieth century that serious and extensive work in rockets began. An American physicist, Dr. Robert H. Goddard, built and fired working rockets that soared many miles into the air. He wrote a long article about how rockets could be used to explore the upper atmosphere, which balloons could not reach. He even suggested that a rocket could be fired to the moon. Though Goddard is now considered the "father of the modern rocket," he was ridiculed for his ideas and his wonderful work was ignored in the United States.

In Europe, on the other hand, there were a number of scientists who recognized the value of Dr. Goddard's work. Among them was Dr. Werner von Braun, a key figure in the development of the deadly German V-2 rocket, which was used to bomb London during World War II. Von Braun's knowl-

27

carried a smaller American-made rocket, the *WAC Corporal*. At the exact second when the V-2 rocket reached its fastest speed, the *WAC Corporal* started its own motor. Thus, it added to the speed it already had. The V-2 rocket dropped off when its fuel was consumed, and the *WAC Corporal* rocket continued going higher and higher. It reached a height of 250 miles above the earth before it started to come down.

The balloon flies like a rocket. As the air rushes out from the neck, the balloon shoots forward.

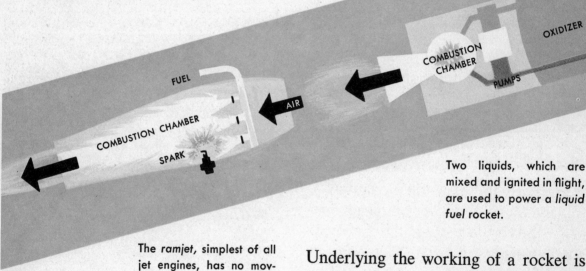

Two liquids, which are mixed and ignited in flight, are used to power a *liquid fuel* rocket.

The *ramjet*, simplest of all jet engines, has no moving parts and must be in motion before it will work.

edge and skill were used after the war by the United States in its rocket research program at the Redstone Arsenal in Huntsville, Alabama.

The first true rocket-propelled space vehicle was fired on February 24, 1949. At that time, the United States Army sent up the first "two-stage" rocket at White Sands, New Mexico. They used a German V-2 rocket, which they had captured during World War II, and it

Why does a rocket fly?

Underlying the working of a rocket is a basic scientific rule — Newton's Third Law of Motion. It is named after Sir Isaac Newton, who was the first man to realize that these rules worked every time and everywhere in the world and even in the universe. Simply stated, this rule says that "for every action, there is an equal but opposite reaction."

Newton's third law explains why a rifle "kicks back" when it is fired. The action of the bullet moving forward out of the gun produces an equal force in the opposite direction. You can test this rule, or law, yourself. Take a balloon and blow it up. When you release it, it will zoom away from you. The balloon flies away because the air inside rushes out of the small opening

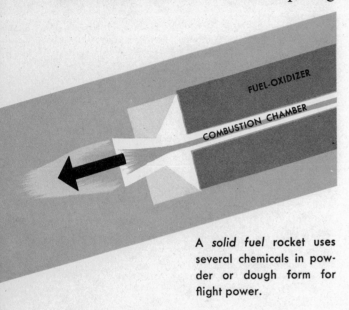

A *solid fuel* rocket uses several chemicals in powder or dough form for flight power.

in the back. In other words, the forward motion is an equal and opposite reaction of the air rushing out the back.

A rocket flies for the same reason. As hot gases, created by burning fuel, escape through the small opening in the rear of the rocket, they create an equal but opposite reaction which drives the rocket forward.

All of you have seen an airplane winging its way through the sky. It is able to do so because we have an atmosphere; that is, nitrogen, oxygen, argon, carbon dioxide and other gases which surround the earth in the troposphere and stratosphere. The airplane needs the air, which is forced over and under its wings by the propeller, or through its jet engines, in order to

Can a rocket fly in outer space?

help the plane rise and move forward. Without the atmosphere, the airplane would not be able to fly, and we know there is no atmosphere several hundred miles above the earth.

A rocket, on the other hand, because it works in accordance with Newton's Third Law of Motion, can operate more efficiently outside the atmosphere than within it. The atmosphere offers resistance, or pressure, against the forward moving rocket. You can test this resistance yourself on a windy day. Take a large piece of cardboard, about

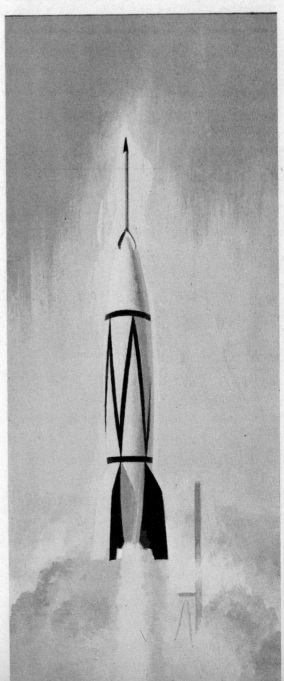

Powerful rockets are used for space probes.

two or three feet square. If you hold it straight above your head and run into the wind, you will find that you feel a pressure against the cardboard; it may even pull your arms back somewhat. But if you hold the cardboard flat, so that only the thin edge faces the wind, you will find little resistance.

There is, however, a different problem which faces the rocket in space. To keep the rocket engine burning, there must be a supply of oxygen. There is oxygen, in gas form, in our atmosphere; it is the same oxygen that we breathe. In space there is no *free* oxygen, as scientists call it. Therefore, the rocket must carry its own supply.

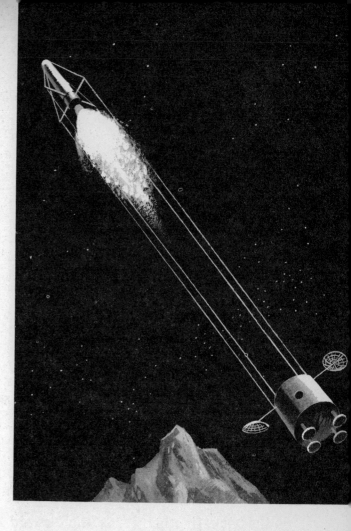

The rocket's thrust, or forward speed,

What fuel does a rocket use?

is created by the escape of hot gases through the rear openings or ports. These hot gases are created by burning fuel within the rocket. Basically, two types of fuel are used in rockets.

First, there is liquid fuel. This often consists of two liquids that are kept in separate tanks. When the two liquids are mixed and ignited, they vaporize or turn to gas. The gases expand when heated, and their only way to escape is through the rear openings. Two of

the liquids commonly used are alcohol and liquid oxygen. The liquid oxygen is called *lox*. The oxygen is needed to support combustion or to enable the mixture to burn in space where no oxygen is available. Another liquid combination consists of high octane gasoline and nitric acid. The nitric acid contains oxygen which permits the mixture to burn.

Second, solid fuels are used in some rockets. This fuel consists of a mixture of several chemicals in powder form. One of the chemicals in the mixture must contain oxygen, which is released as a gas when it is heated. Without this release of oxygen, the mixture would stop burning much in the same way as a candle will stop burning if you cover it tightly by placing an inverted water

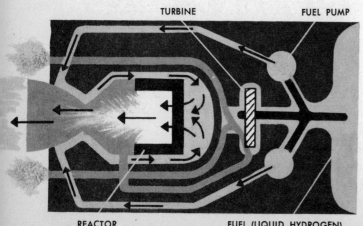

TURBINE   FUEL PUMP

REACTOR   FUEL (LIQUID HYDROGEN)

An atomic reactor and liquid hydrogen are used to power a *nuclear* rocket.

A nuclear-powered spaceship is today's dream of the space age. A nuclear motor is more efficient, developing greater thrust for its size than either liquid or solid fuel rockets. In plans for a nuclear-powered space trip to the moon, Mars or Venus, space engineers hope to use rockets to raise the spaceship above the earth's atmosphere. Here, the bottom stage would be detached and glide back to earth, while the smaller ship would speed ahead on its journey. The nuclear engine would be contained in front, and the men would travel in a gondola suspended by very long cables from the engine. In this way, the men would be better protected from the engine's radioactivity.

glass over it. The flame is snuffed out when its supply of oxygen is gone.

Scientists are experimenting with nuclear power, or atomic reactor engines, to replace the liquid and solid fuels used for rocket propulsion (the force needed to make a rocket fly). In a nuclear-powered rocket, the motor consists of an atomic reactor through which liquid hydrogen is pumped. As the hydrogen is heated by the atomic reactor, it turns into a gas and escapes through the rear ports of the rocket.

Can we use nuclear power for fuel?

A nuclear engine, however, creates very high temperatures — more than 6,300° F. This means that the motor section of a spaceship using a nuclear motor would have to be very well insulated from the rest of the ship, since a spaceman could not stand that extreme heat. Considerable work still has to be done before this type of motor can be used.

The speed necessary to overcome gravity is called *escape velocity*. When a rocket is launched on the earth, it is pushed upward according to Newton's law of motion. It is, however, encountering two other forces. One is the normal pull of the earth, or the earth's gravity. The other is the resistance of the atmosphere.

What is escape velocity?

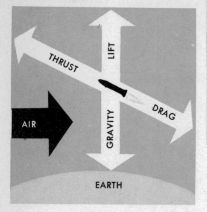

A space vehicle in our atmosphere is affected by four forces. Its *lift* must offset *gravity*; its forward *propulsion* must overcome air resistance or *drag*.

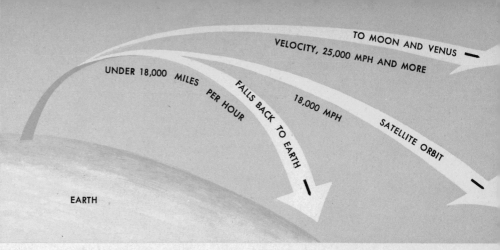

At the speed of 18,000 miles per hour, the space vehicle's lift and propulsion are sufficient to keep it in orbit around the earth. To escape from the earth's gravitational pull, the vehicle must exceed 25,000 miles per hour.

Therefore, the rocket's forward thrust, or speed, must be high enough to overcome these two opposing forces.

A spaceship taking off from another planet or the moon would also encounter gravity, or the pull of that heavenly body. In some cases, there is also an atmosphere. Thus, the escape velocity problem exists elsewhere in space as it does on earth.

On earth, once the speed of 18,000 miles per hour is reached, it is sufficient to offset the pull of the earth, or the gravitational force. At that speed, however, the rocket, spaceship or satellite would remain at approximately the same fixed distance away from earth, circling it as the moon does. We call this going into orbit. The first successful orbital shot was made in October, 1957, when the Soviet Union placed its first satellite *Sputnik I* in orbit around the earth. In January, 1958, the American satellite *Explorer I* was fired into its globe-circling orbit.

If the rocket fails to reach a speed of 18,000 miles an hour, it will not go into orbit, but will return to earth. The spaceship in which Russian cosmonaut Major Titov flew in August, 1961,

reached orbital speed. The Mercury capsules in which American astronauts Commander Shepard and Captain Grissom flew, traveled about 5,100 miles per hour. They did not go into orbit around the earth because the capsules had not reached orbital velocity.

To escape entirely from the earth's gravitational pull, it is necessary to attain a speed of about 25,000 miles per hour. At this speed, the rocket or spaceship would pull free of earth and head out into space. The United States' satellite *Pioneer IV* reached this high speed and left the earth's gravitational pull. Like the planets, it went into orbit around the sun.

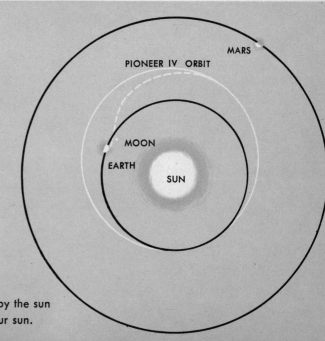

A rocket that misses the moon is attracted by the sun and goes into a planet-like orbit around our sun.

The Techniques of Flight

Who designed the modern spaceship?

One of the earliest attempts at a practical rocketship was made by a German named Hermann Oberth. Because he wrote serious technical books about rockets and space travel during the days immediately after World War I, he was hired by a movie company to be technical adviser for a space-travel motion picture called "The Girl in the Moon."

Although the film was not supposed to be anything but a fantasy, the spaceship Oberth designed for the picture was built very carefully, so that it solved many of the problems a spaceman would encounter in outer space. His spaceship, built over forty years ago, is similar to those designed today.

Hermann Oberth is the man responsible for the rocket countdown that we use today — 10 . . . . 5, 4, 3, 2, 1, fire! He suggested that this be used in the movie because it created suspense. If you have ever watched a rocket countdown, you know how suspenseful that counting can be.

What is orbital flight?

We know that all the planets are constantly moving — rotating on their own axis and, at the same time, revolving about the sun. If you wanted to go from earth to another planet, you would not be able to travel in a straight line. For example, suppose you aimed a rocket at Mars or Venus. By the time the rocket reached the spot at which you aimed it, the planet would have moved along in its orbit, and the rocket would miss its target entirely.

A simple way to explain the complexity of orbital flight is to watch two boys play a special kind of ball game. Usually, if two boys wanted to play catch, they would stand several feet apart and throw the ball back and forth. This would be the same as shooting a rocket from earth to another planet — if the two planets were standing still.

However, suppose we put one boy on a merry-go-round. He is moving in a circle, in the same way that the earth is rotating on its axis. If the boy on the merry-go-round waited until he was directly opposite the other boy on the ground before he threw the ball, the ball would never reach the other boy. As the ball was thrown from the moving merry-go-round, it would not only fly away from the merry-go-round, but it would also loop in the direction the merry-go-round was turning.

Suppose we place the boy on a mov-

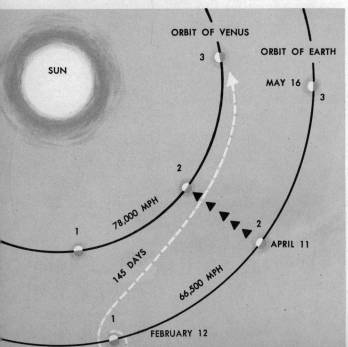

SUN

ORBIT OF VENUS

ORBIT OF EARTH

3

MAY 16

3

2

78,000 MPH

145 DAYS

66,500 MPH

2

APRIL 11

1

1

FEBRUARY 12

On February 12, 1961, the Russians fired a rocket which was to get to Venus, but its radio went dead shortly after blast-off, so it was impossible to determine whether or not a landing had been made. *Mariner IV*, the U. S. space probe, swooped past Mars on July 14, 1965 and transmitted photographs of the surface at a distance of 7,400 miles.

ing train instead of a merry-go-round. If he tried to throw the ball to the boy on the ground when his train was directly in front of the other boy, the ball would never reach its target. The ball would travel out away from the train, but it would also travel in the same direction as the train. It would travel in an arc. This train travel is similar to the earth's revolution in its orbit around the sun.

Actually, we would have to put the boy on a merry-go-round and then put the merry-go-round on a moving train if we wanted to duplicate the two motions of the earth — its rotation and its revolution in orbit.

It would take a lot of skill and practice for the two boys to play catch this way. Of course, in our solar system both planets are moving, and that would mean both boys would have to be on merry-go-rounds that are on moving trains. Imagine how difficult it would then be to play catch!

This is what is involved in orbital flight. Instead of firing a rocket in a straight line, we have to fire it in an arc and make adjustments and corrections for the rotations of both planets and the movements in their individual orbits.

At its nearest point, the earth and Venus are 26 million miles apart. If they were both perfectly still, we could fire a rocket or spaceship that would travel the 26 million miles and land on Venus. This, however, is a theoretical minimum distance.

The actual flight would be much longer, since in space we have the merry-go-round and train movements at very high speeds.

The Space-Age Guide to the Planets on page 48 shows the theoretical minimum flight times from the earth to the different planets. These are calculated on a straight-line flight if the planets were absolutely still and the spaceship were traveling at 25,000 miles an hour.

In reality, however, the flight would take much, much longer, since we would be traveling in an arc.

Orbital flight plans are made by special flight teams composed of astronomers, space technicians, mathematicians, astronauts and other specialists. Any flight to the moon or the planets depends upon the sun's gravitational pull. Despite the earth's sidereal and elliptical motions and the orbital pattern of the moon or a planet, the basic flight pattern recognizes that the sun continues to exert its "pull" on all bodies in our solar system.

How can we navigate in a spaceship?

Even if all the calculations are extremely accurate and the weather and space conditions are ideal, there is always the small possibility that the satellite or spaceship may go astray. The slightest veering off course, over such a long distance, can mean missing the landing target entirely.

Radio telescopes keep in constant communication with the satellite or ship

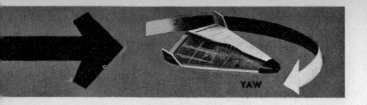

YAW

as it speeds through space. The information received from the many tracking stations is gathered in a control center. Here the information is interpreted with the assistance of a computer, so that fast, accurate answers are assured for all concerned.

To correct the course of a satellite or unmanned spaceship, radio signals are beamed at the ship in flight. These are picked up by the receiver and activate various controls. The firing of compressed air through special vents or the setting off of short rocket blasts will correct faults in flight. This was the method used by the Russians in the flight of their cosmonaut Major Gagarin. The space vehicle in which he traveled could be controlled only by the ground crew and not by the cosmonaut himself.

On the other hand, the United States'

Gemini astronauts were able to control their space capsules by means of instrument panels and on-board computers. The astronauts maneuvered in space at will, docked their spacecraft end-to-end, and positioned the capsules for the final plunge into the earth's atmosphere.

Russian astronauts seem to have much less control of their spacecraft, relying more on control radioed by ground stations.

Only the slightest movement is necessary to alter the course of any rocket or spaceship. Instruments within the ship or on the ground receiving signals back from the ship, can tell if the vehicle is *yawing;* that is, if its nose is swinging from side to side.

Instruments can also tell if the vehicle is *pitching;* that is, if the nose is moving up or down. Once the air is fired through the special vents or a short rocket blast is used, the ship is back on course and on its way.

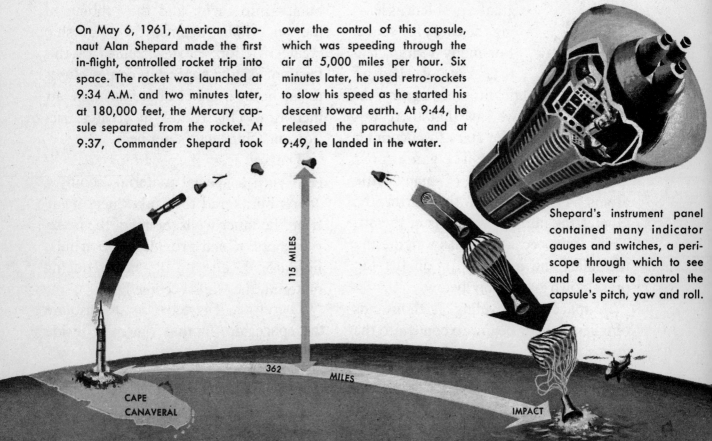

On May 6, 1961, American astronaut Alan Shepard made the first in-flight, controlled rocket trip into space. The rocket was launched at 9:34 A.M. and two minutes later, at 180,000 feet, the Mercury capsule separated from the rocket. At 9:37, Commander Shepard took over the control of this capsule, which was speeding through the air at 5,000 miles per hour. Six minutes later, he used retro-rockets to slow his speed as he started his descent toward earth. At 9:44, he released the parachute, and at 9:49, he landed in the water.

Shepard's instrument panel contained many indicator gauges and switches, a periscope through which to see and a lever to control the capsule's pitch, yaw and roll.

115 MILES

362 MILES

CAPE CANAVERAL

IMPACT

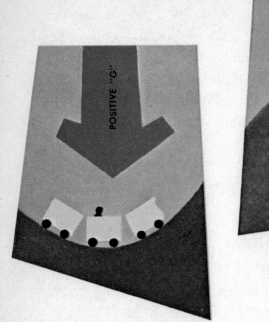

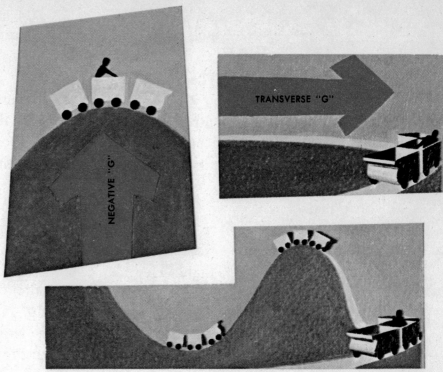

Taking a trip in a roller coaster, you can feel some of the sensations of a space flight. As the coaster comes rushing down, you are subjected to a positive "g" force. Your body feels as if it were being pushed through the seat, and the blood rushes out of your brain. At the top of a fast rise in the coaster, you are subjected to a negative "g" force. You feel as if you will continue going into the air, and extra blood is forced into your brain. When you go around a turn quickly, you are subjected to a transverse "g" force. Your body feels as if it will fly to one side; at this time, the blood in your body is being pushed in the same direction. You, like many pilots and spacemen, can stand this force better than the other "g's."

Returning to the earth from space is as great a problem as leaving the earth for space. For many years scientists have worked to overcome the difficulties of re-entry. As you remember, we saw that there was no air in space. We start to encounter air in our atmosphere. The gases in our atmosphere are made of many little atoms. The closer to the earth, the greater the number of atoms in the air. This is true because air has weight, and the miles and miles of air on the top press down on the air below.

Why is re-entry a problem?

A spaceship traveling at thousands of miles an hour begins to come into the atmosphere. Here it comes into contact with the atoms in the air — it bumps into them, and the rubbing of the air atoms against the spaceship creates friction. Heat is created by this friction. As the spaceship comes closer to earth, the number of atoms in the air increases. This results in greater friction and, thus, in greater heat.

The surfaces of spaceships are covered with a special material, some of which burns and thus takes heat away from the inner walls. Some of the material chars, which provides a good heat insulator. Even with this heat-reducing material, the walls become hot.

Therefore, it is necessary to insulate the spaceship so that the man inside can withstand the heat.

Human Factors in Space Travel

Building a spaceship for space exploration is only part of the problem which we face in space exploration. Preparing the men to travel in these ships is the other part. Every advance in the science of transportation presents a problem and a challenge to man. More than 150 years ago, when the first railroad trains were introduced, there were some people who believed that if man traveled at a speed of more than twenty-five miles per hour, he would die because his body could not stand the shock. While we have come far from this idea, we recognize that space travel does present certain obstacles to man.

What are the dangers to man in space travel?

For example, we know that when men go on long voyages into space, they will be exposed to cosmic radiation, extreme cold, and atmospheres where there is no available oxygen. They will be weightless for months, perhaps years. These difficulties can be solved by proper construction of spaceships. But what about other problems created by extended space travel?

Wearing a specially-made space suit, and lying down for the take-off as well as the landing, help the spaceman to withstand the high "g" pressures.

We know that any real space flight away from earth will take many weeks, even months merely to reach the moon or nearby planets. Will man be able to think and work while he lives in the confined area of a spaceship? If there are several men together in a small ship, will they be able to work together with-

How will man's mind function in space travel?

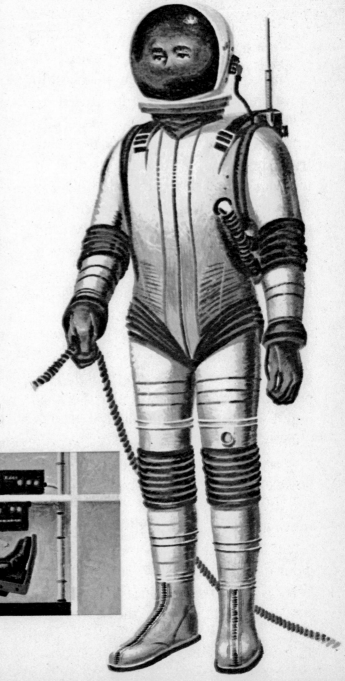

out arguing? Will they become bored or excessively tired?

To find the answers to these and other problems, scientists and medical doctors have created special laboratories in which they study men under the same conditions that are experienced in space. The *Gemini VII* astronauts, Lt. Col. Frank Borman and Commander James A. Lovell, Jr., in their 14-day flight, ate, slept, and worked without any difficulty.

The normal pull of gravity on earth is

What is the g factor?

a force that scientists call "one gravity" or 1 *g*. When a spaceship is taking off, it builds up speed to reach 18,000 miles an hour to go into orbit, or 25,000 miles an hour to escape from the earth. At this time there is an increase in the *g* factor, just as there is when you are standing in an elevator and it starts to rise suddenly and rapidly. The earth is pulling on you just as it pulls on the spaceman, even though the elevator or spaceship is using its power to rise rapidly.

As the *g* force increases, the weight of your body also increases — you feel much heavier. Thus, if you weigh 125 pounds (normal weight under the normal 1 *g* force), you would weigh 250 pounds under a 2 *g* force.

Very high *g* forces can cause you to "black out" or lose consciousness, since the blood cannot circulate properly through your body. Air force pilots are often subjected to forces as high as 7 *g* during a high-speed power dive. However, if they wear space clothing, or stay in a special position, they can over-

come the bad effects of this high *g* factor.

The space suit provides an essential

How does a space suit help a pilot?

safety factor for the spaceman just as it does for high-altitude pilots. It helps to control temperature and air pressure and assures its wearer of a supply of oxygen. The suit is made of a strong, lightweight material that fits the body like a glove. Like the glove on your hand, there is a minute space between the suit and the body in which there is air.

Pressure control is one of the more important reasons for using a space suit. As we go higher above the earth, the air pressure decreases. The normal human being has about five quarts of blood in his body. If you went up to 25,000 feet — about 4¾ miles —

the suit. Furthermore, the oxygen supplied in the suit is temperature-controlled so that no matter how cold it gets outside the spaceship — or inside — your body remains comfortable.

To help overcome the high g forces to which the spaceman is exposed during take-off, he has to use a special seat. This seat is something like a bed, so that his body appears to be lying down in the ship. In this position it is easier for his heart to pump the blood to all the parts of his body as compared with a standing or sitting position.

To prepare the space traveler for the **How does a spaceman train for the high g factors?** high g factors he will experience in take-off and in landing, he is trained in a *centrifuge* (CEN-tri-fuge). This is a large machine with a rotating arm to which a model cabin of a spaceship is attached. The motor of the machine rotates the arm at faster and faster speeds, and the spaceman in the cabin is thus subjected to increased g pressure. Some of the astronauts have been subjected to a force as high as 40 *g*. If the man normally weighed 200 pounds, his body would weigh four tons or 8,000 pounds under this force. Many spacemen have been able to take this pressure for short intervals and still remain conscious.

Have you ever taken a ride on a roller coaster? Have you **How does "weightlessness" affect man?** ever been in an elevator when it started to descend suddenly and quickly? If you have,

A controlled dive of a conventional plane puts this man in a weightless state. His reactions are carefully checked.

above the earth without a space suit or without a pressure cabin in a plane, the oxygen in your blood would bubble out as a gas. The normal five quarts of blood would need the same space as fifteen quarts on the ground. At 50,000 feet, the oxygen gas would expand further, making the space needed for the five quarts almost the same as eighty-five quarts on the ground. You can readily see that your body would virtually explode as the blood expanded.

In addition, the space suit is connected to several tanks in the spaceship. One tank maintains the proper air pressure; another supplies the oxygen; still another takes the harmful carbon dioxide, which you exhale, out of

you've experienced "weightlessness." The sensation we feel when the parts of the body press against each other for support is the feeling of weight. Once this pressure is removed, we feel weightless. In technical language, this is known as a *zero g force*.

For some people it is an uncomfortable feeling. They are so upset that they cannot think of anything else; nor can they react properly when they are required to pull a lever or read an instrument dial. All they want is to "land," or to feel normal again. For others, weightlessness appears to be no problem. They glide through "space" feeling as if they were swimming underwater. They can move and react normally.

Weightlessness is encountered in space flight. To help spacemen to become accustomed to this feeling, they are taken in fast-flying jet planes that simulate a roller coaster ride through the air at high speeds. Both the American and Russian astronauts were able to function normally during their weightlessness period while flying through the lower level of space.

Although men are able to become accustomed to weightlessness for short periods of time, we do not know how men will react if this feeling is continued for many weeks, or months, or perhaps years. Medical doctors and scientists are studying this problem in order to find the answers.

Flying at high speeds in a spaceship creates many problems for the spaceman. One of these is the time he takes to react to signals from the ground or warnings from his instrument panel. In the many studies made by doctors and psychologists of people's reactions, it has been found that it takes about three-tenths of a second to react. For example, if you put your hand in some very hot water, it would take about three-tenths of a second before you pulled it out. That is the time it takes for the signal from nerves in your hand to reach your brain — for your brain to decide what to do — and for your brain to order your muscles to pull your hand away. This three-tenths of a second is called *normal reaction time*.

How important is "reaction time" in space travel?

In space flight, the spaceman is subjected to a feeling of weightlessness or excessive *g* forces. He is also affected by the noise level or complete silence within his ship, as well as other factors. The question is: Can he maintain his normal reaction time?

To find this answer, doctors and scientists have experimented with animals and they have tested men. When Ham, the astro-chimpanzee, flew in his rocket spaceship in February, 1961, he was traveling at a speed of 5,800 miles an hour, or 1.61 miles per second. A man in the same ship would have flown almost half a mile *before* he could react to any signal.

We have learned much from Ham and other chimps. They were taught to push different levers, depending upon which signal appeared on a screen. When they pushed the correct lever, they were rewarded with a banana-flavored pellet. If they made a mistake, they received nothing. The chimps learned quickly and one of them was able to push the right lever at the rate of one hundred correct movements in a single minute — more than one each second. The chimps made far fewer mistakes than many human beings who tried the same test.

We have found that men can maintain their normal reaction time under space-flight conditions in the laboratory. We have also seen that the American astronauts and the Russian cosmonauts were able to do so for their flights. The question still remains: Can man continue his normal reaction time during a prolonged space flight of several weeks or months?

That question will have to be answered in the future.

In February, 1961, an astro-chimp named Ham became the first earthly creature to operate controls in a space capsule.

Into Space by Stages

We have already sent men into the lower reaches of space, and we have fired space **Why are space stations needed?** vehicles that have both landed on — and orbited — the moon, as well as others that have orbited the sun. Nevertheless, these are only the initial probes into space. While scientific instruments can do a better job than man in obtaining and recording space information, man wants to do the exploration himself. To make this possible, it is necessary (1) to obtain as much scientific data as possible by first using instruments; (2) to provide maximum safety for man in space to assure his safe return; and (3) to provide the spaceman with "steppingstones" into space.

These steppingstones, or space stations, are necessary since they will provide extra protection for spacemen and permit the more efficient use of space vehicles. The station could provide protection by eliminating some of the dangers and difficulties of landing a returning spaceship directly on earth. It would also make possible the refueling of ships in space, since a considerable amount of fuel is consumed getting the ship into orbit. With added fuel, it would be safer to make longer space probes in manned ships.

Space stations, circling about 500 miles above the earth, would have additional uses. They would be weather observation posts, providing more accurate and more detailed weather information for long-range forecasts. They would act as radio and television relay stations so that we could beam live television broadcasts to all parts of the world. This would eliminate the necessity of telephone lines encircling the earth. The station would also act as a dock wherein spaceships could be repaired.

While plans for space stations progress, we have been carrying out phases of a moon exploration program. One of these, identified as *Project Ranger,* was designed to obtain close-up pictures of the near side

How will moon sites be chosen?

of the moon, which in turn would be used in selecting a landing site for astronauts. Nine *Ranger* spacecraft were fired at the moon. *Rangers I* and *II* went into low-altitude (100-mile) orbits around the earth. *Ranger III* missed the moon and went into orbit around the sun. *Ranger IV* curved around the moon and crashed into the moon's hidden side, sending no pictures back to earth. *Ranger V* also missed the moon and went into orbit around the sun. *Ranger VI* crash-landed precisely in the lunar Sea of Tranquillity, where it had been aimed, but sent back no pictures. *Ranger VII* sent back 4,304 photographs of the moon before it crashed into the Sea of Clouds. *Ranger VIII* swept over the mountainous area not far from the center of the near side of the moon as it closed in on the Sea of Tranquillity, taking 7,137 photos before crashing. *Ranger IX* crashed into the crater Alphonsus, after sending back 5,814 photos of the moon.

The *Ranger* program was followed by *Project Surveyor,* in which 5 of 7 camera-carrying spacecraft were soft-landed on the moon. The *Surveyors* took and transmitted back to earth thousands of pictures, some taken from only a few inches above the moon's surface.

The *Prospector,* which will be able to move along the surface of the moon like a tractor, is the third exploration vehicle in the program. Its movement, however, will be limited to a small area of the moon because of the irregular surface of that body. Falling into one of the moon's crevices or chasms could wreck the instrument capsule.

Our nearest neighbor in the solar system, the moon, is the most logical spot for man's first space exploration.

How will a manned moon-flight be made?

The moon is 2,160 miles in diameter, roughly about one-fourth as large as the earth. At its *perigee* (PER-i-gee), or nearest point to the earth, it is 221,593 miles. At its *apogee* (AP-o-gee), or farthest point from the earth, it is 252,948 miles away.

The space vehicle that will carry astronauts to the moon is the three-part *Apollo* spacecraft. The upper part, the command module, houses three astronauts and the instruments.

Below the command module is the service module carrying supplies to support life in space, radar, and a 22,000-pound-thrust rocket and its fuel.

Lowermost is the lunar module, the part that will land on the moon.

The spacecraft will be boosted into space by a 7,500,000-pound-thrust *Saturn V* rocket. By the time the rocket has reached about 114 miles, its first two stages will have burned out and dropped off. The third stage will put the *Apollo* into orbit around the earth. From orbit, the astronauts will blast off on a flight path to the moon. Then the astronauts will separate the third stage from the command and service modules, turn the latter two around, and dock them with the lunar module still within the rocket's third stage.

Upon arriving at the moon, the spacecraft will go into orbit and the lunar module (or "Bug") will descend to the surface with two of the astro-

RANGER

SURVEYOR

PROSPECTOR

PROJECT RANGER LAUNCH

Artist's view of the moon.

nauts, who will explore and then rejoin the third astronaut in the orbiting command and service modules. When all three astronauts are back in the command module, they will fire the rockets of the service module, leaving the lunar module behind, and depart for the earth. Close to earth, the service module will be left behind, and the astronauts will land in the command module.

With just a small telescope we can see many details of the moon's surface. But even the most powerful one can give information about only one side of the moon. Its rotation on its axis and its revolution about the earth are synchronized so that only one side of the moon faces the earth at all times.

What will man find on the moon?

The surface of the moon which we see has four distinct characteristics. First, there are the lofty mountains. The Leibnitz and Dorfel Mountains in the southern part of the moon exceed 30,000 feet. Second, there are the broad dark plains or "seas" of the moon, which are visible with the naked eye. Scientists believe that they were once seas of lava, but that they are now a hardened crust.

The third and most outstanding feature of the moon are the craters. They are very deep and very wide and can be found almost everywhere on the surface. The Clavius crater, for example, is 17,000 feet deep and 145 miles in diameter. Finally, there are the rills. These are long, very deep crevices that are sometimes a mile or more wide at the top.

The dark side of the moon, that which we never see, was first photographed by the Russian satellite *Lunik II* in 1959. In 1967 and 1968, orbiting spacecraft sent to the moon by the United States took thousands of detailed pictures of both sides of the moon. As a result, we know that the hidden side of the moon looks very much like the side we have always seen, having mountains, "seas," craters, and rocks.

The surface of the moon, as you can imagine, is not an easy place on which to land a spaceship. There is always the danger of coming down in a rill, on the steep wall of a crater or in the rugged mountains. Furthermore, the surface of the moon is covered with volcanic and meteoric dust. The *Surveyor* spacecraft have shown that this dust is firm enough to provide solid support for a lunar module.

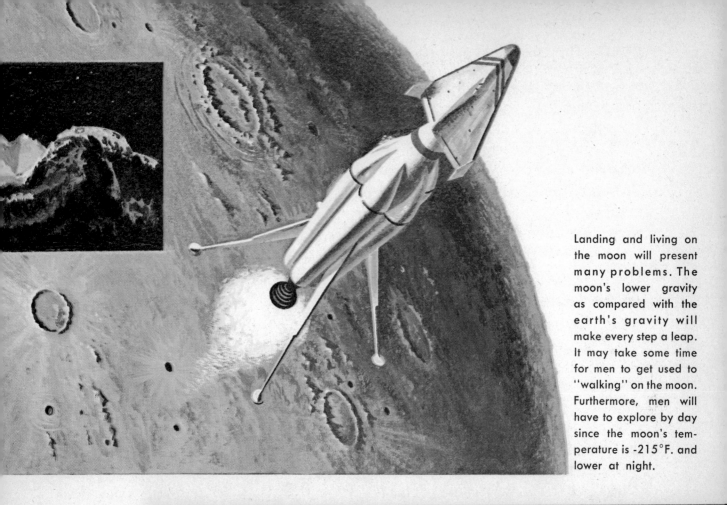

Landing and living on the moon will present many problems. The moon's lower gravity as compared with the earth's gravity will make every step a leap. It may take some time for men to get used to "walking" on the moon. Furthermore, men will have to explore by day since the moon's temperature is -215°F. and lower at night.

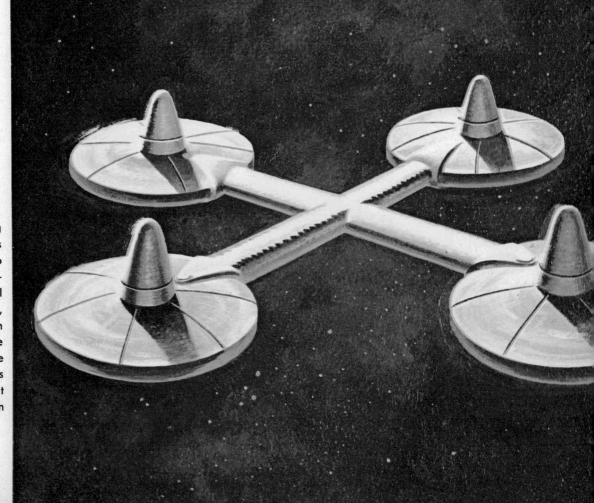

Space stations orbiting the earth can act as steppingstones into space. They will be assembled from material rocketed into space, which will continue in orbit as the men put the station together. The one illustrated here is the Douglas Aircraft Company's "Mexican Hat Space Station."

The atmosphere of the moon is another riddle. Although there are some who believe that the moon has no atmosphere, others contend that it has a thin atmosphere, composed of argon gas and other gases that have been released by the decay of radioactive potassium. In either case, they all agree that there is no oxygen in the air for a man to breathe.

When man goes to the moon, he will need to bring along **Can man live on the moon?** food, water and oxygen. He will find that the moon's gravity is only about one-sixth the gravity of the earth. A 200-pound man would weigh only 33 pounds on the moon, and when he walked, he would be able to practically leap through the air because of this low gravitation pull.

A man on the moon will be exposed to extreme temperature changes. It reaches over 135° F. in some areas, and several astronomers now believe that the temperature goes as high as 250° F. At the other extreme, the low temperature reaches −215° F. We are not certain what the temperature condition will be on the dark side of the moon, but many believe that it is about −300° F. at the warmest.

The lack of an atmosphere or even the very thin atmosphere on the moon creates another problem. The moon is being constantly showered with micrometeorites (very small meteorites), which pass through the space above the moon without meeting any resistance from the air or atmosphere. On earth, any micrometeorites or even meteorites burn up because of the friction that is created as they pass through our atmosphere. On the moon, however, these small particles pass through and land without difficulty. Some of the larger micrometeorites, traveling at high speeds, may puncture the skin of a spaceship, the roof of a moon spaceport or even a man's space suit. Special suits will be needed for this protection.

Some space experts recommend that we build underground bases on the moon. However, the moon's surface contains large amounts of metal ore and rock, so that underground construction may be too difficult, if not impossible, without heavy machinery.

Considerably less fuel is needed for a spaceship to return **Why is the trip back to earth easier?** to earth than is required for a trip from the earth to the moon. There are two reasons for this. First, because the moon's gravitational pull is much less than the earth's, less force is needed to put the spaceship into the air. Second, this weaker gravitational pull means that the spaceship will travel for a shorter time before it leaves the moon's gravity field and enters the earth's gravity field. Actually, escape velocity on the moon is only slightly over 5,000 miles per hour as compared with 25,000 miles per hour needed to escape from the earth. Furthermore, within less than five hours, the spaceship leaving the moon would be within the earth's gravity field.

Once the ship reaches this point, it can begin its "fall" to earth because it is being attracted, or pulled, by the earth's gravity. The ship's speed would increase as it falls toward earth and reach 25,000 miles per hour. Once it enters the earth's atmosphere, it would be slowed somewhat by the air resistance. It would be necessary to use auxiliary rockets or blasts of compressed air to slow the ship to 18,000 miles an hour, the speed at which it could then orbit around the earth.

If there were a space station 500 miles up, the spaceship would be able to "land" there, and the spacemen could return to earth in another ship. Otherwise, the moon-ship itself would begin its slow descent, and the men would parachute into the sea in a capsule, as the *Mercury* and *Gemini* astronauts did, or onto solid ground, as Russian cosmonauts do.

Close Looks At The Planets

While American astronauts and Russian cosmonauts

What did Mariner find out?

are straining every nerve in a race to the moon, the moon journey will be only a very small step into space. The moon is only 238,856 miles from the earth, and a space journey to the moon would take only 3 days. A journey to our nearest neighbor, the planet Venus, would take 3½ months when Venus is closest to earth. A journey to our other neighbor, Mars, would take 7½ months when Mars is closest to earth. Before men land on these planets, scientists want to know much about what the surfaces of these planets are like. Some attempts to get this knowledge have already been made.

On August 27, 1962, the United States launched the spacecraft *Mariner II* toward Venus on a mission to find out some things about the thick layer of clouds that covers that planet. On December 14 *Mariner* passed 21,648 miles from Venus and radioed back information about the temperatures of the clouds and possibly of the surface of Venus. *Mariner* found that the surface temperature of Venus may be as high as 800° Fahrenheit. This is far too hot for living things we know on Earth to exist on Venus. The base of the clouds that cover Venus had a temperature of 200° Fahrenheit and the outer surface of the clouds had a temperature of 60° below zero, Fahrenheit. Also, *Mariner* reported that Venus does not have a magnetic field like that of the earth, nor does it have belts of radiation, like the earth's Van Allen belts.

In 1964 and 1965 the Russians made at least two unsuccessful tries to send a spacecraft to fly past Mars and send back data. On November 28, 1964, the United States, too, aimed a spacecraft, *Mariner IV*, at Mars. On July 14, 1965, this *Mariner* passed within 7,400 miles of Mars' surface and sent back to earth the first photographs of Mars that were not taken from the earth.

These closeups revealed that Mars has a surface pitted with craters, much like the moon's surface. These craters were probably made, like most of the moon's craters, by meteorites striking the surface.

Mariner also found out that Mars has a very thin atmosphere. This means that astronauts would have to wear pressurized suits to live on Mars.

On March 2, 1966, the Russians an-nounced that two spacecraft, *Venera 2* and *Venera 3*, had made space journeys to Venus. *Venera 2* passed within 15,000 miles of the planet on February 27, and *Venera 3* crash-landed on Venus. But neither craft sent back any information because their broadcasting equipment went dead.

The United States plans to send to Mars spacecraft which will land and take samples of the soil, look for plants or animals, and seek other information. Then, perhaps in the 1980's, astronauts will land on Mars.

Space-Age Guide to the Planets

Planet	Mercury	Venus	Earth	Mars	Jupiter	Saturn	Uranus	Neptune	Pluto
Distance from the Sun (millions of miles)	36.0	67.2	92.9	141.5	483.9	886.0	1783.0	2791.7	3670.0
Theoretical Minimum Time to Reach Planet from Earth	83 days	45 days		58 days	1 year, 8 months	3 years, 5 months	7 years, 5 months	12 years, 2 months	12 years, 2 months
Diameter (miles)	3,100	7,700	7,927	4,200	85,750	71,150	32,000	27,600	3,700
Time to Complete One Orbital Revolution Around the Sun (measured in Earth time)	88 days	225 days	365.26 days	687 days	11 years, 314 days	29 years, 168 days	84 years, 7 days	164 years, 285 days	248 years, 146 days
Length of Day (measured in Earth time)	88 days	225 days	23 hours, 56 minutes	24 hours, 37 minutes	9 hours, 50 minutes	10 hours, 14 minutes	10 hours, 49 minutes	15 hours, 40 minutes	16 hours
Surface Gravity (measured in terms of 1 g on Earth)	0.35	0.88	1.00	0.38	2.64	1.17	0.92	1.40	0.16
Weight of a Man on the Planet if He Weighed 200 Pounds on Earth	70	176	200	76	528	234	184	280	32
Escape Velocity (miles per hour)	9,700	23,000	25,000	11,500	133,200	79,200	49,320	57,600	22,000
Temperature on Surface	—460°F. to 780°F.	—4°F. to 140°F.	—90°F. to 136°F.	—130°F. to 85°F.	—215°F. average	—240°F. average	—300°F. average	—330°F. average	—345°F. average
Number of Moons	0	0	1	2	12	9	5	2	0